String Time Joggers

14 pieces for flexible ensemble

Kathy and David Blackwell

Contents

This symbol indicates the CD track numbers for each piece. The top number indicates the complete performance, and the bottom number the accompaniment alone. A tuning note (A) is located on track 29.

Viola

Sea Suite

1. Shark attack!

© Oxford University Press 2007

Printed in Great Britain

OXFORD UNIVERSITY PRESS, MUSIC DEPARTMENT, GREAT CLARENDON STREET, OXFORD OX2 6DP
The Moral Rights of the authors have been asserted. Photocopying this copyright material is ILLEGAL.

2. Barrier Reef

Very calm ♩ = 60

3. Cap'n Jack's Hornpipe

Jazz Suite

4. Simple syncopation

5. Feelin' blue

Slow and moody ♩ = 68

6. Broadway or bust

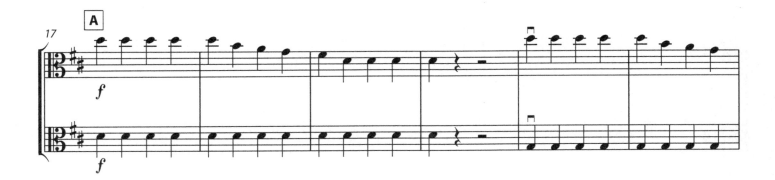

Jamaican Suite

7. Tinga Layo

(Part 1 and Harmony)

West Indian Trad.

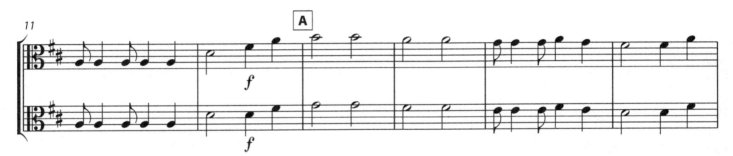

7. Tinga Layo

(Part 2)

West Indian Trad.

8. Jamaican lullaby

Jamaican Trad.

Gently flowing ♩ = 104

9. Kingston Calypso

(Part 2)

Sunny ♩ = 130

 9
○
23

9. Kingston Calypso

(Part 1 and Harmony)

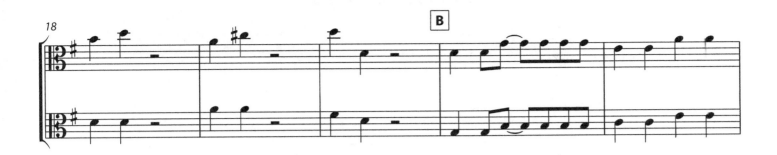

Hollywood Suite

 10. Spy movie 2

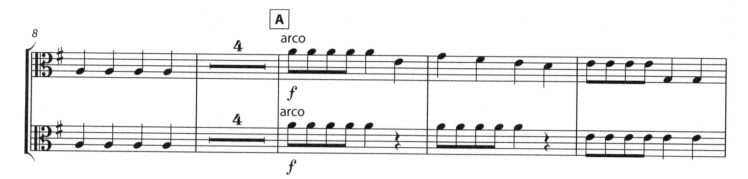

11. Sad movie

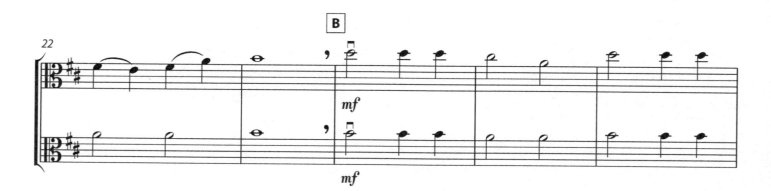

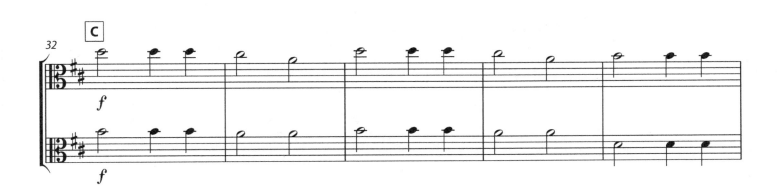

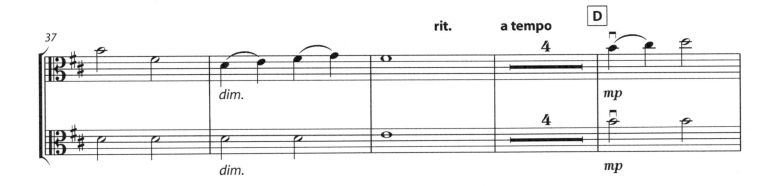

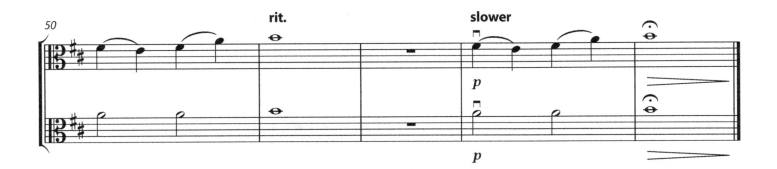

12. Action movie

Marching ♩ = 112

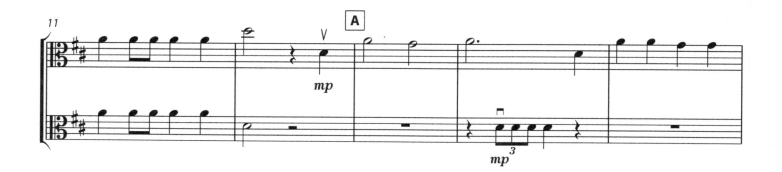

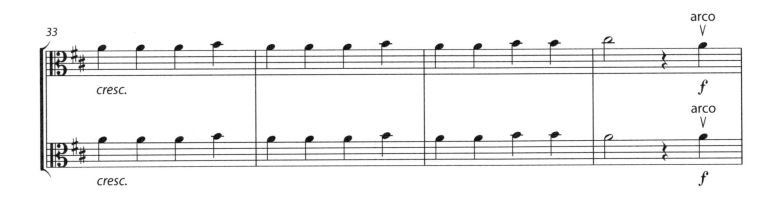

Extras

13. Cowboy song

MELODY

14. Banuwa

MELODY

African Trad.

OSTINATO